Introduction

This book is about people like you and me. The trouble is that there are rather a lot of us and our numbers are increasing so fast that we may destroy the planet we live on sometime in the next few centuries if we are not careful. At the present rate of growth the population of the world would double in 40 years. In the time you have taken to read this far the number of humans living on Earth has increased by 50. If this trend were to continue at the same rate, by the end of the 26th century each person would only have one and a half square metres of land – standing room only. In the developed countries we have come to regard cars, fridges and televisions as necessities, and naturally people all over the world would also like to own these things. But in making them we are using up the Earth's limited supply of raw materials.

Industry and everyday life all generate some kind of pollution which is beginning to harm the environment. If the number of people requiring a better quality of life goes on increasing, the Earth's materials will be used up more quickly, pollution will grow worse and there will not be enough food for us all. For nearly all the time that human beings have lived on the Earth, there have not been enough of us to have any real effect on the world around us. The small amounts of pollution were easily absorbed by the natural surroundings and though there may have been local overcrowding there was more than enough room for all. Now this situation has changed. The Earth can still support more people but there must be a limit and we are reaching it too quickly.

Already we are aware of the problem and in many parts of the world educational, medical and birth control programmes are helping to reduce the numbers of babies born. But is the population explosion already out of control?

3

CHAPTER ONE

WHY WORRY ABOUT MORE PEOPLE?

As long ago as 1798, the English economist, Thomas Malthus, wrote about the problem of increasing population. He was worried that there would not be enough food for the growing population which was then less than one billion, but beginning to grow faster. It took almost all of the history of the world for the total population to grow to one billion in about 1830. Then, less than a hundred years later, it had reached two billion, adding a third billion in about 30 years and a fourth in another 15 years. It is now over five billion and growing by about 230,000 more people every day. A look at the history of the world's population, and its different growth rates around the world at different times, reveals the magnitude of the problem.

△ Londoners swarming to work like insects.

▽ Thomas Malthus 1766-1834

304

THE POPULATION EXPLOSION

JOHN AND SUE BECKLAKE

GLOUCESTER PRE
London · New York · Toronto · Sydr

CONTENTS

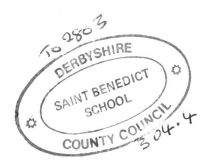

▷ So many people live on the tiny island of
Singapore that overcrowded housing is
inevitable.

Population figures
When talking about population we usually use figures expressed as rates: birth rate, death rate and growth rate. These are useful because they can show simple comparisons for different countries or different times. The birth and death rates are just the numbers of births or deaths for every thousand people each year. If there are more births than deaths the population will grow and vice versa. The difference between the birth and death rates gives you the growth rate for the total population, or the number of extra people per year for every thousand.

Sometimes percentage rates are used, which is just the growth or the number of births or deaths per year for every hundred people. When figures are given for the population in the future these are only informed guesses.

Growing slowly

Intelligent human beings appeared on the Earth about 100,000 years ago and for a great deal of this time they lived primitive lives, their numbers increasing very slowly, if at all, to begin with. The birth rate was fairly high but so was the death rate. Many children died very young and those that survived to become adults could not expect to live nearly as long as we do today. There were many reasons for this high death rate; wars, famine and malnutrition, but most of all diseases. Some were dramatic like the bubonic plague, or Black Death, which swept across Europe in the middle of the fourteenth century, killing more than one in every four people.

For thousands of years the population grew slowly. It approximately doubled between the birth of Christ and the year 1500 with a rate of increase less than 0.1 per cent per year. Compare this with the annual rate of population growth now which is between 1.7 and 1.8 per cent. There were occasional sharp increases in local areas, for instance Italy's population grew rapidly at the time of the Roman Empire, only to fall again later. Then about 1750 the world population started to grow faster and this growth got more and more rapid, until it was doubling in only about 35 years. Only in the last ten years has it begun to show signs of slowing down at last.

The Industrial Revolution

We are not certain why the "population

explosion" began between 1750 and 1800, but this was soon after the start of what we call the Industrial Revolution, and there may be a link. Before then industry had been limited to small factories run by windmills, waterwheels or even muscle power. Then the Industrial Revolution brought steam engines to power new machines in larger factories, which were mostly built near a source of coal or iron ore. At about this time improvements in methods of agriculture and the introduction of machines on the farms meant that more food could be produced on the same amount of land by fewer workers. People moved from the countryside to the towns and cities where the factories provided many new jobs. Slums rapidly appeared around the cities to provide accommodation for the flood of incoming workers. Thus the Industrial Revolution brought about enormous changes in lifestyle for most people. It started in Britain but quickly spread across Europe and North America, to a large part of what we now call the developed world.

Why did the population grow so fast?

The industrial revolution changed people's lives but did it have an effect on the population growth? To begin with people drifted to the cities where they lived in absolute squalor. Death rates were much higher there than in the countryside, and in England there was a slow increase in the birth rate between 1700 and 1800. However the Industrial Revolution made the country more wealthy. Athough not everyone became rich and many of the working classes were still very poor, there emerged a prosperous middle class. Gradually the average wealth for the whole country increased. Living conditions slowly began to improve in the 19th century, and increased output of food from farms reduced malnutrition, both of which helped to lower the death rate.

At the same time as progress in industry and engineering, came progress in medicine. Doctors began to understand that the cholera and typhoid epidemics that killed so many people were caused by bad sanitation and could be prevented.

△ Developing industry has led to increased air pollution seen here.

△ An "average" family in the developed world.

Vaccinations against smallpox, and cures for many of the killer diseases were eventually found and people began to live longer, healthier lives. In Britain the death rate fell slowly between 1750 and 1850 and then began to drop fast. It roughly halved from 23 deaths per thousand in 1850 to 11 per thousand in 1930, resulting in a huge increase in the numbers of people. In England and Wales there were 9 million people in 1800, rising swiftly to 18 million in 1850 and to 32 million in 1900. This was due almost entirely to the drop in adult death rate. It was not until the beginning of this century that the death rate for young children fell and this in turn added to the population as more children grew up to have their own families. Thus the last century saw a huge growth in the populations of the industrialised countries which is now being repeated in the rest of the world.

These population trends were virtually unaffected by the two world wars of the twentieth century. Despite the fact that an estimated 50 million people died in the Second World War (civilians and soldiers), this did not significantly influence trends in population.

Population and War
The effects of wars on the population is less than you may think. In fact at the end of the First World War (1914-18) which killed about 8 million soldiers in Europe, a flu epidemic killed more than twice as many people. Wars now kill civilians also. In the Second World War (1939-45) almost as many civilians as soldiers died.

△ Vaccines keep children healthy.

A divided world

Today the world's population is growing at two different rates, very slowly in industrialised countries and much faster in the less developed parts of the world. Let us look at why there is this difference.

Child workers of the past

We have seen that the Industrial Revolution was followed by a huge increase in population growth because the death rate dropped as prosperity increased, while the high birth rate remained steady. But the reasons for having lots of children gradually disappeared. With fewer children dying young it was not necessary to have lots of babies to ensure that a few survived to adulthood. As countries became more prosperous, pensions and social security systems were introduced to help support elderly and retired people, and to care for the sick. So it was no longer essential to have children to look after you in old age.

Industrialisation also changed the way people lived, more worked in factories and offices and fewer on farms where children could help with the work. Laws were also passed to limit child labour in factories and mines. Children stopped being a practical and financial benefit to the family and began instead to be a financial burden. The birth rate gradually began to drop.

Today the populations of most countries in Western Europe and North America are growing very slowly if at all. Here, the population explosion is over, defused by increased prosperity, but this is not so in the rest of the world.

△ These children weaving carpets in Pakistan are already earning money and helping support their families.

◁ In developed countries children are not allowed to work, but learn and play while young.

8

△ In Mali it may take the whole family all day to collect firewood.

▽ An Indian family includes young and old.

Population in the developing world

Many of the developing countries of Africa, Asia and South America, are now in the first stages of this process. The population is now growing very fast, as it did in Europe in the last century. Nearly two billion people, over a third of the world's population, live in India and China, both with growing populations. The United Nations Organisation expects each of these countries to have about 200 million more people (roughly three times the present population of Great Britain) by the end of the century. Other countries like Kenya and Syria have even faster growing populations. Their increase of over 4 per cent per year does not sound much but it means that their numbers are doubling every 17 years. The birth rate will remain high while parents need large families to help with the work in the mostly rural communities, and to care for their parents when they are too old to work. In many places religious beliefs have also encouraged large families and still do, and sons are often valued more highly than daughters. However all this is beginning to change.

Development in many of these countries is bringing better education, medical care and a higher standard of living, all of which leads to lower birth rates. In addition the status of the woman is beginning to rise, giving her more influence over the size of the family. But even if the birth rates start falling very soon there are so many babies being born now, and surviving to have their own children, that the population will go on increasing for many years yet. We cannot predict exactly when this growth will stop but the population of the whole world will probably be over ten billion before it levels off at more than double its present level.

Where are all the people?
Do you think the world is overcrowded? When you are sitting in a traffic jam in Los Angeles, London or any other major city in the world you would be justified in thinking that it is. Many places like the shanty towns that have grown up around cities like Bombay or Mexico City, or even popular seaside resorts in summer, are grossly overcrowded. However there are still remote places where you can travel for days without meeting anyone. If we were all spread out evenly over the Earth there would appear to be plenty of room for all of us.

Aid to development
In the developing countries the number of people has grown enormously in the last few decades, mainly because of medical help from the developed world. Immunisation has reduced infant deaths from childhood diseases and the death rate has fallen much more rapidly than it did in the developed countries during the last century. However, most people are still very poor and need many children to help support the family. Thus birth rates are still high. In 1982, aid and investment in developing countries from the United Nations, other countries and large multinational companies was nearly $40 billion.

△ The most enduring aid that the developed world can give is education.

△ Hong Kong is already very overcrowded.

△ The Arctic is empty but could we live there?

Satellite pictures from space of the dark side of the Earth show the many bright lights of the towns and cities but between them are huge dark areas where people are very few and far between. Why do people all flock to the cities?

In the past, farming the land to provide food needed lots of people. As more machines were used in farming, fewer people were needed, while at the same time the population was growing faster and faster. With no work available in local farming communities, people tended to move to cities to find work to support themselves but there were not enough jobs or houses for them all and so slums spread around many large cities with all the problems caused by overcrowding. Some areas become overcrowded because they attract people by their prosperity like Hong Kong, where there is so little land space that tall buildings of crowded flats are the only way to house all the people. If all the land in the world was shared equally between everyone now, we would each have an area of about 30 thousand square metres. This sounds a lot but many places like the ice caps and the deserts are not suitable to live on. Even without these areas there is still plenty of land to support us all now, but what about the future? Technology may be able to help us by providing food more efficiently and enabling us to live in less hospitable places – where it is very hot or very cold or even under the sea. But this would only give us temporary relief if we cannot manage to stop the population explosion.

Population

Human beings appeared over a hundred thousand years ago but life then was very difficult and short and the numbers of people grew very slowly. By the birth of Christ two thousand years ago there were still only about 250 million people altogether, roughly the same number of people living in North America today. This doubled to 500 million in 1,600 to 1,700 years and doubled again to 1,000 million (1 billion) in about 200 years. At the present rate the population is doubling approximately every 40 years. If the Earth is about half full now it will only be about 40 years before it becomes completely full. Then, in another 40 years or less, we would need a whole new planet to accommodate the extra people. This is called exponential growth. The world population was growing exponentially but has now started to slow down. But even if it slows down to a growth rate of 1.5 per cent per year by the year 2000, it will still mean 90 million extra people each year.

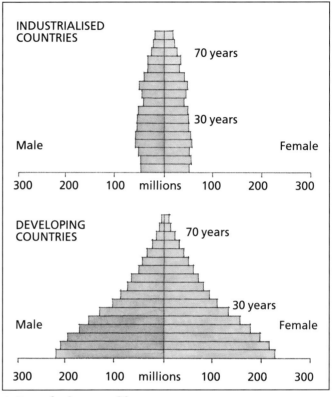

△ **Population profiles**

In the developing countries high birth rates mean more young people than older ones. Where birth rates are low the numbers of young and old are not very different.

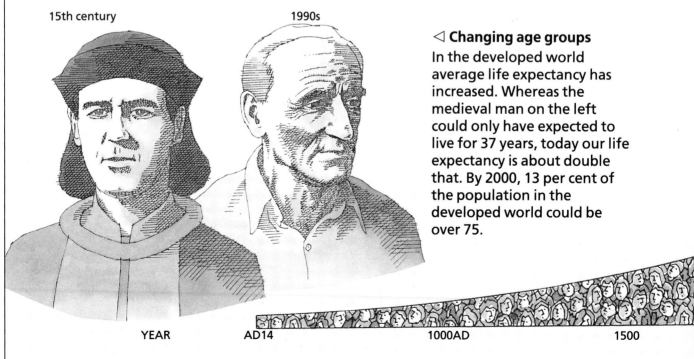

◁ **Changing age groups**
In the developed world average life expectancy has increased. Whereas the medieval man on the left could only have expected to live for 37 years, today our life expectancy is about double that. By 2000, 13 per cent of the population in the developed world could be over 75.

15th century   1990s

YEAR   AD14   1000AD   1500

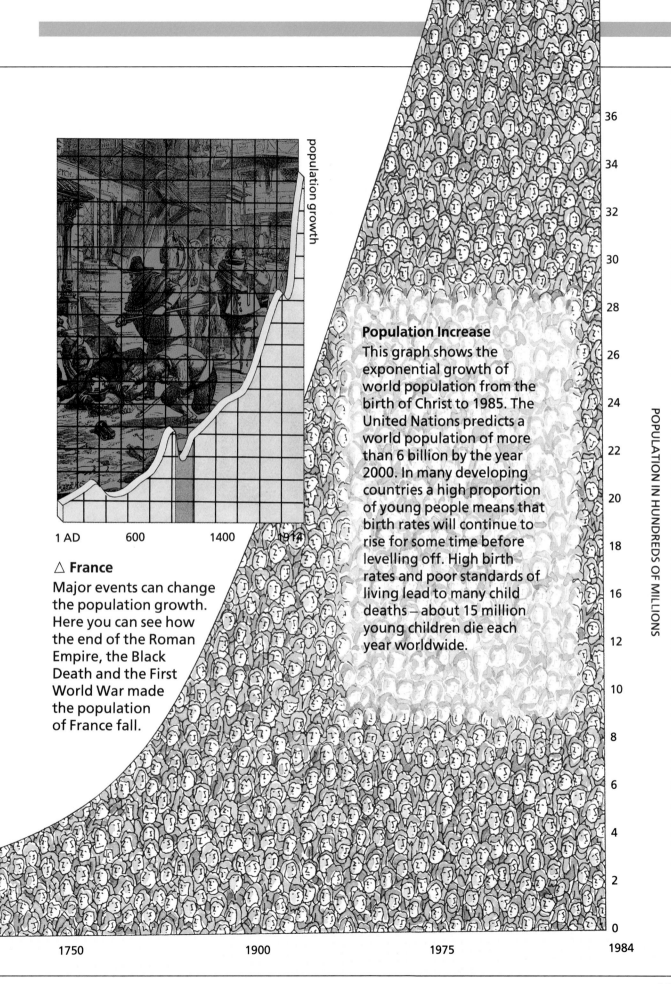

population growth

1 AD   600   1400   1914

△ **France**
Major events can change the population growth. Here you can see how the end of the Roman Empire, the Black Death and the First World War made the population of France fall.

Population Increase
This graph shows the exponential growth of world population from the birth of Christ to 1985. The United Nations predicts a world population of more than 6 billion by the year 2000. In many developing countries a high proportion of young people means that birth rates will continue to rise for some time before levelling off. High birth rates and poor standards of living lead to many child deaths — about 15 million young children die each year worldwide.

POPULATION IN HUNDREDS OF MILLIONS

36
34
32
30
28
26
24
22
20
18
16
12
10
8
6
4
2
0

1750   1900   1975   1984

CHAPTER TWO

MORE PEOPLE – MORE PROBLEMS

Can the fertile areas of the world produce enough crops to feed a population that will double in about 40 years if its present rate of growth continues? We are using up the Earth's valuable natural resources to produce roads, buildings and luxurious "necessities". We do not know how long our raw materials will last or how easily new reserves can be found. We need supplies of energy, for heating, lighting and to run our homes and industries. We are constantly using up fuels which cannot be replaced.
Another problem is pollution. We allow our waste products and poison to escape into the air, rivers and seas. Already there are so many of us that Nature cannot absorb or neutralise all the pollution we make.

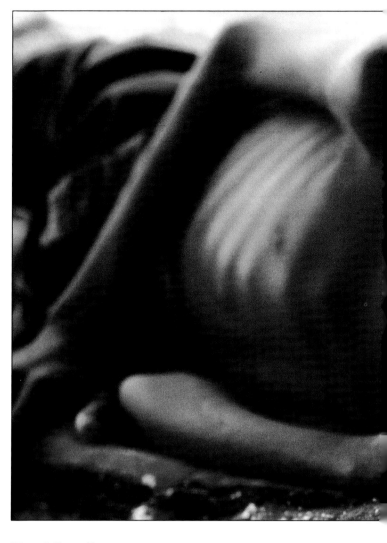

Food for all
News of terrible famines in parts of Africa, killing thousands of people, might make you think that we cannot grow enough food for everyone now. But you would be quite wrong. Famines happen partly because food is not evenly distributed, (some countries have too much and others too little) and partly because local wars or political conflicts prevent farmers growing their crops, and transporting food to where it is needed. Since the 1940s farming has become much more efficient and the amount of food produced has increased faster than the population has grown. Between 1970 and 1980 the world food production grew on average by 2.5 per cent per year while the population growth was between 1.8 and 1.9 per cent per year.

△ There is no shortage of wheat in the US.

◁ A failed harvest brings famine in Ethiopia.

This "green revolution" happened because new strains of wheat and rice were bred to give higher crop yields and to resist diseases.

Problems of the green revolution

Such progress brought problems with it. The artificial fertilisers and pesticides which are frequently used to boost growth can also cause pollution problems both from the industrial process when they are made, and on the land when they are used. Chemicals called nitrates from the fertilisers are washed out of the soil into the rivers which supply our drinking water. Nitrate pollution also destroys the habitats of the plants, fish and animals normally living in the rivers. Breeding better plants for crops means that fewer different varieties of crops

Famine and debt

Many developing countries are in areas where the land is so poor it is a struggle to grow enough food for all the people. In countries near the Sahara desert, like parts of Ethiopia, if there is not enough rain and the harvest fails, there may be widespread famine. But they cannot always use all the land to grow food for themselves. Often countries have to grow "cash crops" for export to repay their debts.

are used, so an attack by a new disease could prove catastrophic.

We are producing enough food now but how much more can we produce? Agricultural experts are optimistic; they are confident that we can grow enough to feed double our present population. The challenge will be to increase food production without increasing pollution from fertilisers and pesticides. We will also have to take care of the farming land so that it does not lose its fertility as we demand higher and higher crop yields from it. Topsoil, the fertile part of the soil, is now being lost more rapidly with these new intensive farming methods. If the soil is overworked it turns into dust which just blows away in the wind, especially if natural breaks like hedges, and tree cover of the woods and forests, have been destroyed. If the population continues to grow we will reach a point when the Earth cannot provide enough food for us all.

Power hungry world

Food is not the only resource under threat from an increasing population. In the industrialised world, huge amounts of energy are consumed to maintain a lifestyle that uses technology extensively. Power stations all over the world burn fossil fuels – coal, oil and natural gas – to make electricity to power factories, and to light and heat our homes and run our domestic appliances. Cars, planes and trains also use fuels made from oil.

But there is only a limited amount of these fuels in the Earth. It took a million years for nature to produce the amount of fossil fuels that we burn each year in the whole world. Not only are we using up these precious resources at an ever increasing rate but also when we burn them we release polluting gases into the atmosphere. Oil spills, from drilling rigs and tankers carrying oil around the world, are occurring more frequently. We spoil the countryside with slagheaps and open cast mines when we take coal and minerals from the ground. The world production of energy and therefore consumption of fossil fuels has grown much more rapidly than the population. Since 1900 our use of fossil fuels has increased 30 times, while the world population has increased three times. So population growth has not directly

△ Dealers at a stock exchange

created an energy crisis, but the demands of people for a higher standard of living will.

Uneven use of resources

However the whole world does not benefit equally; over 70 per cent of the energy produced is used in the industrialised nations where only 20 per cent of the world's people live. Far greater problems will undoubtedly occur as the developing nations also become more industrialised. Now they use only a tiny share of the world's fossil fuels but naturally everyone would like a higher standard of living and this means using more energy both to make and use things like cars and electrical goods. *If all the people in the world now were to use energy at the same rate as those in the industrialised countries we would need nearly four times more power.*

We are already looking for ways of producing energy, including solar, wind and nuclear power, that are less polluting and do not use up non-renewable natural reserves. It would also help if we were much more careful with the energy we have. In the past energy has been so cheap that little

△ Pollution from a conventional power station.

△ A gold mine in Brazil

effort was made to use it economically. A great deal of energy is wasted because of badly insulated houses, inefficient industrial processes and the use of private cars instead of public transport.

Disappearing raw materials
Industry needs raw materials to produce all the things we use in everyday life. Some materials are renewable like cotton, rubber and wood, which come from plants and trees. These are harvested and replanted for a new crop. Many materials however are not renewable. These include the minerals containing metals, and the fossil fuels we burn for energy. The Earth contains a fixed amount of these, and we are using them up faster and faster, as the rate of industrial growth increases.

Already some renewable materials like hard woods are being used faster than they are being replaced, and eventually the non-renewable materials will run out. This will not happen just yet; apart from a few, very rare materials, that are already very expensive, most of the mineral deposits that we now know about in the

Earth's surface will last for over 50 years, if used at the present rate. By then we will probably have found more reserves although these will be more difficult and expensive to extract because the more obvious sources are found and used first. We will also have found substitutes for some materials.

The problem is that we are not likely to go on using materials at the same rate. Industrial output has been growing much faster than the population. Since 1900 while the population has increased three times, industrial output has gone up 50 times, mainly for the benefit of the one fifth of the world's population living in the industrialised countries. With the numbers of people in the developing countries growing raw materials will be used up more quickly as they seek to improve their standard of living.

Problems of waste
The developed world is very wasteful, throwing things away when we no longer want them or when they wear out, but much could be recycled to conserve the

17

supplies of raw materials. This would mean sorting out rubbish so that metals and other valuable materials can be collected and used again instead of being wasted. However, not all materials can be recycled. Some, like the fuels burnt to provide energy, are destroyed when they are used. Recycling would also partly solve the vast problem of waste disposal. One estimate shows that when the world population doubles, as expected by the middle of the next century, it could produce 400 billion tonnes of solid rubbish every year, enough to cover the whole of Greater London with a layer 100 metres deep!

People and pollution

Everyone of us causes pollution just by throwing away rubbish, burning fuels for warmth and energy, and with our sewage.

Long ago before the population began to rise dramatically, nature could cope with human waste. The carbon dioxide gas from burning fuel is absorbed by plants, solid waste decays naturally to provide food in the soil for living things, and small amounts of liquid waste are easily absorbed into the water of the rivers and oceans. However as long ago as the Middle Ages towns and cities began to be polluted with rubbish in the narrow streets. Open sewers, harbouring deadly diseases contaminated local water supplies. Coal burning fires filled the atmosphere with soot and polluting gases. Then the Industrial Revolution started and more industrial pollution was added to human waste. Nature found ever increasing pollution more difficult to absorb. London and other major cities were once well known for

△ In Brazil an open sewer spreads disease and pollutes the water supply.

smogs caused by smoke, which probably killed thousands of people each year. Rivers like the Rhine became so dirty with toxic waste dumped directly in them from factories, that most fish were unable to live in their polluted waters.

Today laws have been passed to prevent many of the more obvious kinds of local pollution; London smogs have disappeared and the River Thames, for example, is now clean enough for fish again. But we are still left with more insidious kinds of pollution. Fewer factory chimneys belch out soot and smoke but they release gases making acid rain which blows across continents to kill trees in the forests and fish in the lakes of other countries. Burning petrol in more and more cars and producing energy from fossil fuels releases carbon dioxide gas into the atmosphere which, along with methane

from natural gas, is gradually warming the whole planet and changing the climate. We have only just realised that CFCs used in spray cans and refrigerators are destroying the ozone layer, letting more dangerous ultraviolet radiation from the Sun reach the Earth.

Pollution is another global problem caused by the combination of population growth and industrialisation. Undeveloped countries contribute very little to world pollution at present, but are suffering nonetheless from problems caused by the industrialised world, for example, the dumping of poisonous wastes from some unscrupulous industries. Although it may be expensive, industry will have to be much more careful about what it releases into the atmosphere and rivers, seas and land, or we will slowly poison our whole planet.

△ Acid rain from Europe's industry is killing the forests in Germany and Scandinavia.

◁ The famous London smogs have now disappeared.

CHAPTER THREE

STOPPING THE POPULATION GROWTH

The population of the world is already growing much too fast and must be slowed down and stabilised. Otherwise wars, worldwide famine, or poisoning from pollution will reduce the population for us. At the present growth rate of about 1.8 per cent per year, the number of people in the world will double by about the year 2030. Even at half today's rate there would be 40 million more people to feed every year. We are already trying to slow this increase. Many countries, with the help of the United Nations Organisation, are encouraging people to limit the size of their families. This seems to be working; over the past ten years the world population has been increasing at a slower rate. Our ultimate aim must be no growth at all.

△ Overcrowding is common in cities.

Families – large or small?

In many of the developed countries of the world populations are increasing very slowly, if at all, yet not much more than a hundred years ago they were growing as fast as any today. This has happened because people in developed countries now prefer to have smaller families. Their children are not expected to contribute much financially to the family, and until they are old enough to earn a living, they are very expensive to keep, even for the basics like food and clothing, let alone the luxuries.

The reasons for having large families have disappeared and the birth rate has fallen. Some people now choose not to have any children at all, though most have two or three, just enough to keep the population at a steady level.

of birth control to prevent unwanted babies. There is education to explain their use and people can choose the method that suits them best. This relies on good medical care always being available to advise and to check on health generally and to diagnose the occasional side effects that may occur. Although a few countries have religious objections to some or all forms of birth control, generally it is taken for granted that a couple will plan their family and only few births are not planned or welcomed. Even though most people are free to choose the size of their families, there are pressures that influence them. Financial pressures tend to keep families small, while religious pressures can encourage larger families. The governments of some developed countries even encourage parents to have more children. These include East and West Germany, France, Hungary, Romania and Bulgaria. Other influences are external events like wars. At the end of the Second World War the birth rate rose in Britain, and again in the 1960s when the children born after the war grew up and had their own families.

In much of the developing world this change is still to come and their populations are growing fast. We would expect this growth to slow down naturally and eventually level out as in the developed world. However it is very difficult for developing countries to raise their standard of living while their populations continue to grow. There is not enough money to pay for better education, health care, food and housing.

Choosing to have children in the West
One of the reasons for the slow population growth in developed countries is that parents are able to choose how many children to have and when to have them, or even not to have children at all. In most of these countries there is a range of methods

△ Some women choose to go out to work.

21

Birth control

There are many ways to prevent babies being born but they are not all suitable or acceptable to everyone around the world. It is not enough just to make these methods available, they must be accompanied by information to explain their advantages and how to use them. In the developed countries where medical help is never far away, the most familiar contraceptives are probably the condom and the hormone pill. More drastic measures include sterilisation, a small operation leaving the man or woman infertile and unable to have children. This is often used when a couple already have all the children they want. An abortion removes the foetus from the woman before birth, usually very early in the pregnancy. This is probably the most controversial method of preventing unwanted births however it has been common around the world throughout history, and with adequate medical supervision is often acceptable today.

Education and Health in developing countries

It is not always easy, suddenly, to introduce birth control into societies where for centuries children have traditionally been seen as a blessing. Families are usually very close knit, living and working together, with grandparents often looking after the small children while the parents work. However things have begun to change; with improved health care all round the world people are living longer, healthier lives. Now education is following, explaining the advantages of smaller families and how the numbers of children can be limited, without

22

undermining the values of each society. This basic education must be available to women as well as men. In many societies education has been limited mainly to the men, and they have taken the decisions in the family as well as the community. The woman's role has been in the home looking after the husband and children, and she has been regarded more as property than as an equal partner. With improved general education women become able to contribute more both in the home and as wage earners.

Better medical facilities are also an essential part of any successful family planning programme. Medical care must be brought to each village preferably by local people with medical training who understand local problems. The health of the whole family is then improved so the children are more likely to grow up strong and healthy. This also relies on sufficient food being available, which is one obvious advantage of a smaller family with fewer mouths to feed and more food for all.

Learning to read
Many people are illiterate, and almost all of them live in developing countries. Where there is better education and more people can read and write, the birth rate tends to be lower. Already the percentage of illiterate adults has fallen from 59% in 1960 to 41% in 1980. But the world's population is growing so fast that the number of illiterate people rose by about 90 million in that time.

△ Local health clinic in Kenya

◁ Women being educated in Nicaragua

◁ Far left: An Indian poster showing the advantages of family planning

Birth control programmes around the world

It was the major non-governmental organisations, like the International Planned Parenthood Federation (IPPF), that pioneered family planning services around the world. This effort intensified after the Second World War and in 1969 the United Nations Fund for Population Activities (UNFPA) was formed, offering financial and technical assistance to countries wishing to run birth control programmes.

The UNFPA has worked closely with the non-governmental organisations and has been involved with many countries world-wide to help stop the runaway population growth. They have met with varying degrees of success because it depends greatly on the commitment of individual governments, who must provide the improved health care and education to make birth control programmes successful. The status of women must be improved, educating them so they can share in decision making, especially the size of the family. Birth control programmes must offer methods that suit individual societies, particularly in remote areas where medical facilities are often far away.

Half the world's population live in Asia and it is here and in parts of Africa and Central and South America that the population battle must be fought. The situation is not the same in all developing countries. Some have shown little interest in population policies and birth control, like Kenya and some Arab countries, whose populations will double in less than 20 years at the present rate. Others, like China, the country with the largest population in the world, have made enormous efforts to limit their numbers, and have reduced their rate of population growth.

China's children

China's population, which was already the world's largest for a single country, grew steadily, from 542 million in 1950 to 891 million in 1973. Immediately after the Second World War her leaders did not think it was necessary to limit the size or

FAMILY PLANNING—A BASIS NATIONAL POLICY OF CHINA

◁ In China huge family planning posters are used to persuade people that small families are happy families.

▷ Newborn Chinese children are cared for in a nursery. Parents are encouraged not to have more than one child.

growth of the population, believing it would not affect China's economic development. After years of war, the new communist government had to rebuild the country. The Chinese leader Chairman Mao Tse-tung also felt that a large, poor population would more readily welcome socialism. But by 1957 it became obvious that the population was growing too fast. Birth control campaigns were started, but faltered almost immediately and a later campaign was hindered by the Cultural Revolution, which started in 1966.

Finally in 1972 China set herself a very ambitious target; to limit the population to less than 1,200 million by the year 2000. To achieve this they embarked on a thorough programme of education and persuasion aimed at only one child per family. This would eventually mean that there would be no brothers, sisters, aunts, uncles or cousins in Chinese families. The education programme spread information on modern contraceptives, which are all available free of charge, as are abortions and sterilisation.

Another measure was to raise the minimum legal age for marriage, which is now 22 years for a man and 20 for a woman, and the same law required married couples to practise family planning. It is estimated that 70 per cent of Chinese couples use modern contraceptives. Improved health care and nursery facilities were used to persuade parents to have only one child, together with tremendous moral pressure both from the state and the local community. Huge numbers of unwanted pregnancies were ended by abortions; in 1984 there were 18 million births in China and 9 million legal abortions.

These measures would not be acceptable in many countries but they are very successful in slowing China's population growth. The birth rate has more than halved since the late 1960s as has the population growth rate, which is now 1.4 per cent per year. Though even at this rate, estimates say that there will be about 200 million more Chinese people by the year 2000. China hopes to reduce her growth rate still further to zero by 2030 – only 40 years from now. However birth control programmes have not been so successful in other countries.

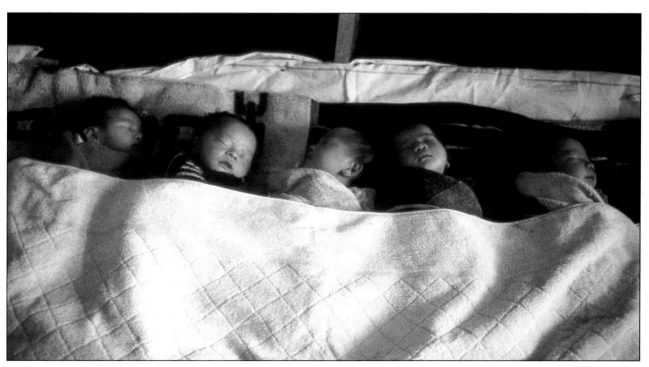

Egypt

Egypt is a country where the birth control campaign has failed to reduce the birth rate. It is a medium sized country in the Middle East, a region where very high population growth is not uncommon. However Egypt was the first Arab state to have a national family planning policy and the first Muslim country in which religious leaders agreed that Muslims could practise birth control. Family planning clinics were set up as early as 1955 and expanded in 1965 to make contraceptives available all over the country from shops as well as health centres. This was accompanied by an education campaign and schemes to improve women's education and employment opportunities. The only problems were that abortion was illegal, and religious authorities did not really approve of sterilisation or indeed any form of birth control. In 1972, with a population of nearly 35 million, Egypt aimed at reducing the growth rate from 2.5 per cent per year to 1 per cent per year by 1982.

This has failed completely; by 1982 the growth rate had not changed at all and births had actually risen from their 1972 level. The reason for this failure could lie in the very strong traditions and religious beliefs, but it is probably due to insufficient enthusiasm for the birth control campaign generally. Egypt's population is now expected to be over 65 million by the year 2000. It is not a rich country and its economic development will be severely hampered by a huge population.

Western Europe

The situation in the industrialised countries of Western Europe is a complete contrast to that in Egypt. Most of these populations are now growing very slowly and some are even beginning to fall. This levelling off has not

△ This clothing completely covering Egyptian women is a symbol of their status in a Muslim society.

◁ Very few Egyptians will be able to buy cars because while their population continues to grow they will remain poor.

been due to a particular effort to encourage birth control methods, though these, combined with good education and medical care, are now taken for granted. It is simply that lifestyles have changed. Since 1950 fewer young Europeans have been getting married and those that did, married later and chose to have fewer children. Some married women choose a career instead of children while fewer exercise their right to have larger families. In many European countries young people are given information about birth control, sometimes in schools, with the aim that every baby should be planned and wanted by its parents. So the birth rate has been falling fast, and if this continues, the overall population will begin to fall in the 1990s. It is not the same all over Europe; in some countries like the Republic of Ireland where there is religious opposition to birth control the birth rate is higher. However in others, like West Germany, Austria and Switzerland, the number of people is already falling. One researcher has estimated that, in the unlikely event of birth rates continuing to fall at the present rate, by 2090 there will only be half as many people as there are now in Europe.

△ In developed countries education is a right.

△ Older people need more care.

An older population

However a falling birth rate and stable population brings its own problems. In the past young people greatly outnumbered the elderly. Working people between the ages of 16 and 65 produced enough wealth to support the retired population. However as people live longer and fewer children are born the working population is shrinking while the retired population is growing. It is also becoming more expensive to support them because as people get older they need more hospital or nursing care.

In West Germany, where the birth rate is so low that the population is actually decreasing, people are being encouraged to have more children so that the country can afford to look after its older people properly. This policy may be right for West Germany at the present time, but it is rather insensitive to attempt to increase your population while most of the world is desperately trying to reduce theirs.

Population problems can look different depending on each country's point of view – they will have to be solved globally with all the countries working together.

The global situation

The map below shows the increase in population around the world in 1989. The size of the human figure indicates the average growth in different parts of the world, though the actual growth can vary dramatically from country to country as these examples show:

Less than 1% – West Germany, USA, and Australia
1 to 2% – China, Jamaica and Indonesia
2 to 3% – Brazil, Bangladesh and Mexico
3 to 4% – Algeria, Iraq and Zimbabwe
Over 4% – Kenya and Gaza

Some coutries, often in Central America, Africa and Asia where the populations are growing fast, cannot support the people living in them now. By the year 2000 there may be over 1.5 billion people in these countries.

Stability

People may move to escape natural disaster or as a result of political changes. This can affect a country's population profile. The photograph shows East Germans crossing the Berlin Wall to the West – will the movement of people between these countries change their population profiles?

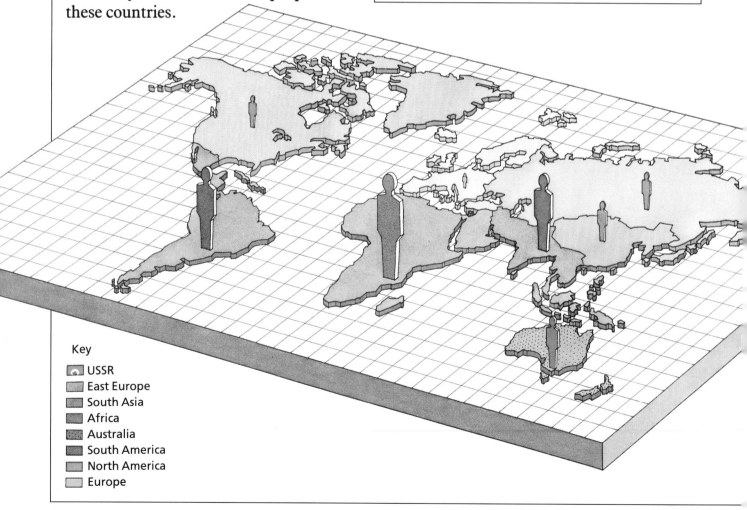

Key
- USSR
- East Europe
- South Asia
- Africa
- Australia
- South America
- North America
- Europe

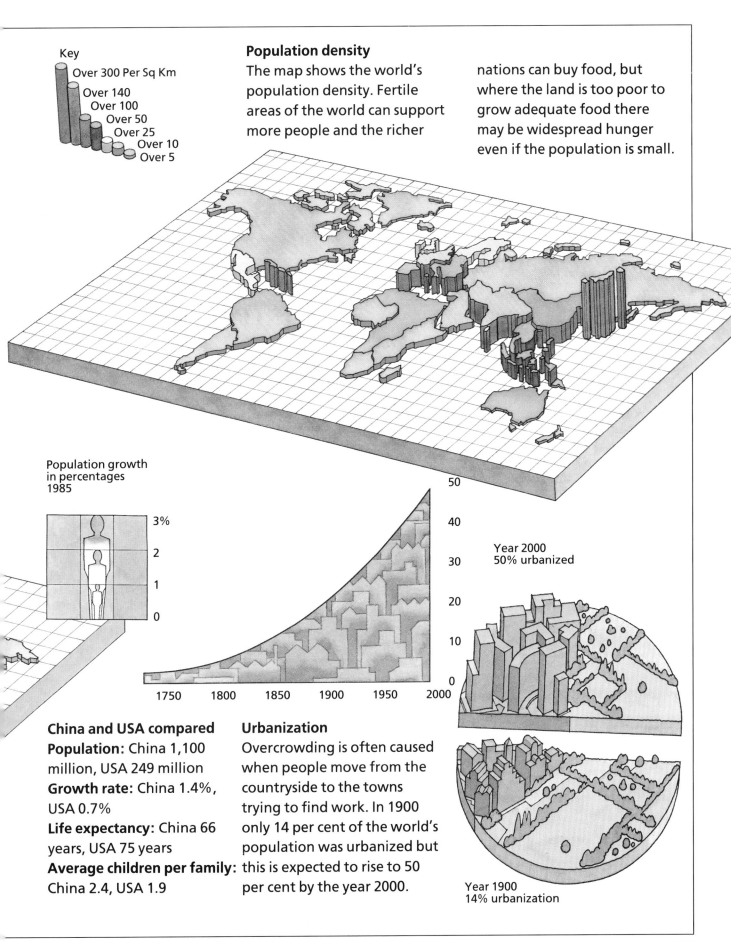

Key
Over 300 Per Sq Km
Over 140
Over 100
Over 50
Over 25
Over 10
Over 5

Population density

The map shows the world's population density. Fertile areas of the world can support more people and the richer nations can buy food, but where the land is too poor to grow adequate food there may be widespread hunger even if the population is small.

Population growth in percentages 1985

3%
2
1
0

50
40
30
20
10
0

1750 1800 1850 1900 1950 2000

Year 2000
50% urbanized

Year 1900
14% urbanization

China and USA compared

Population: China 1,100 million, USA 249 million
Growth rate: China 1.4%, USA 0.7%
Life expectancy: China 66 years, USA 75 years
Average children per family: China 2.4, USA 1.9

Urbanization

Overcrowding is often caused when people move from the countryside to the towns trying to find work. In 1900 only 14 per cent of the world's population was urbanized but this is expected to rise to 50 per cent by the year 2000.

CHAPTER FOUR

CATASTROPHIC POPULATION CONTROL?

What will happen if we do not manage to stop the population explosion? Perhaps famine in some parts of the world will reduce the numbers by starvation. Another killer could be pollution if it is allowed to increase unchecked.

In the past plagues have reduced population drastically and modern medicine cannot cure or prevent all diseases. In the future, nuclear war could have such catastrophic effects that it could reduce the population. If the population grew beyond its ability to feed itself, we could find ourselves at war, fighting over food or other essential natural resources or even a space to live in. Any or all of these unpleasant possibilities could eventually stop the population growth if we cannot or will not do it for ourselves.

Natural disasters

In Bangladesh disastrous flooding has made many thousands of people homeless, without food, water, shelter and often clothing. Without proper water supplies there is the danger of widespread disease. People wait for food that has been supplied by relief organisations.

So far the world can supply enough food for all and the needs of victims of natural disasters can be met. But war, political instability and greed often rob the victims of food and medical supplies that were intended for them. Should the population explosion go unchecked, then the world may not be able to supply enough food for all and natural disasters may cause even more loss of life.

◁ Getting rid of the rubbish from cities like London and New York is becoming a problem. Much of today's rubbish does not decay naturally. Open rubbish dumps encourage rats which spread disease and buried rubbish can produce explosive gases like methane.

Persuasion or enforcement?

We would like to be able to persuade and encourage everyone that smaller families can be healthier, better fed, wealthier and a good idea in general. But if this does not work, can we force people to limit the number of children they have? Would you like to live in a state where you have to apply for permission to have a baby and are only allowed a maximum of two children? There might be compulsory sterilisation after you have had your two children or compulsory abortions for all unplanned pregnancies. It might be necessary to wait for someone to die before permission is given for another child to be born. Another possibility could be compulsory euthanasia with elderly people only being allowed to live to a certain age before being killed. None of these measures are acceptable to us now, but are they worse than war, famine or plague restricting the population?

△ Will people live here in your lifetime?

Migrating to new worlds

In the past when overcrowding became a problem and a country could not support a larger population or was running out of resources, people could emigrate to a new country. America and Australia both became "new worlds" colonised by people from Europe. Now however there is nowhere left on Earth for people to escape to, except perhaps to underwater cities built on the ocean floor. Our "new worlds" will have to be out in space, on other planets or space cities orbiting the Earth. These space cities would be self-sufficient, taking an inexhaustible, pollution free supply of energy directly from the Sun, in the same way that we may all get our energy in the future. Their raw materials would come from the Moon or the asteroids and they would grow their own food. However they could not be built in time nor could they accommodate enough people to solve the population problem now. This also applies to permanent colonies on the Moon or the nearby planets, though it is possible that we may be able to use minerals from the Moon or the asteroids when those from Earth begin to run out. These may be attractive possibilities for the future but they will not solve the immediate problem on Earth.

△ They will solve the world's future problems.

△ Wind supplies some of our energy needs.

Is population growth a good thing?

Not everybody thinks that we should worry about our population growth. There are people who argue that human beings are our greatest natural resource, and instead of trying to stop population growth we should be encouraging everyone to reach his or her full potential. Looking at the recent successful record of science, medicine and technology in overcoming many of our problems, they think that we should foster human inventiveness to solve any future problems. Of course we are already using science and technology in our development of different sources of energy which produce less pollution and do not depend on our limited supply of fossil fuels, and in our efforts to reduce pollution and waste. Science can also help in developing more efficient ways of producing more, or exploiting new, sources of food. Not least it can help us find more efficient and convenient methods of birth control.

This is one point of view, but most people who study population issues believe that it is essential to use all the means available to try to stop the population explosion. Human beings are undoubtedly a very important natural resource and we should make the best use of their potential. However, if the population continues to grow exponentially, all our resources, human and technological, will be fully stretched just struggling to provide basic essentials for all. Surely it would be better to try and stabilise the population and then use technology to improve living standards especially for those who are now underprivileged.

Are we winning?

Although the world's population is still growing at a frightening rate, there are now signs that it is beginning to slow down. The population growth rate, which rose sharply to a maximum of 2 per cent per year around

1970, has begun to fall again slowly but steadily, reaching 1.7 per cent in 1985. There has been an even more dramatic drop in the fertility rate worldwide, which fell from 5.0 for the years between 1950 and 1955 to 3.9 for 1975-80. This drop was greatest in the developing countries where the fertility is higher anyway. In the developed countries, although the drop in fertility rate was not so large, it is now about 2.05. This is significant because it is approximately the level at which the population remains steady, our eventual aim worldwide. This looks very hopeful but we have not won the battle yet. Although the growth rate is beginning to decrease, the total numbers are still increasing rapidly. In 1960 when the world population was only 3 billion, the growth rate of 1.8 per cent meant 54 million extra people each year. However in 1985 there were 4.8 billion people in the world and although the growth rate was less at 1.7 per cent, this added 80 million people to the total.

Another problem is that the numbers will not stabilise immediately after the world fertility rate has dropped to the required level but will go on growing for some time. According to United Nations estimates, if this level is achieved by 2035, it would take another 60 years for the population to level off, by which time it would have reached 10 billion.

Stability

It should be possible to achieve a stable population of 2 to 2.5 times the present total by the middle or the end of the next century. However this cannot happen before we have provided everyone worldwide with at least the basics of sufficient food, housing, medical care and education. This will require a more equitable sharing of all the Earth's resources and much more careful management of the whole planet. We will still have the problems of pollution but we must learn to manage them.

△ The United Nations organises practical help for people in Sudan.

GLOSSARY

birth control prevention of unwanted children by naturally or artificially preventing fertilisation of eggs or the development of the egg in the womb.

birth rate the number of babies born each year for every thousand people. The average now for Europe is 13 and for Africa 45.

cash crop a crop grown purely to earn money by sale on international markets, and does not provide food for people in the country producing it.

contraceptive a birth control drug, device or method.

death rate the number of deaths for every thousand people each year.

developing countries countries with little industry and mainly rural economies. Average income per head is low and health and education provision is often poor, though conditions vary widely.

exponential growth growth which speeds up with time, starting slowly then getting faster and faster. World population has been growing exponentially. At first it took thousands of years to double then hundreds and now less than forty years, though it has begun to slow again.

fertility rate average number of children a woman will have in her lifetime. A rate of just over 2, called the **replacement level**, keeps the population steady.

industrialised countries countries with economies based on industry where factories provide more jobs than agriculture. Usually the income per head is high and provision of health care, education and social services is good.

Industrial Revolution development of manufacturing industries starting in the 18th century in Britain and quickly spreading to Europe and North America and accelerating throughout the 19th century.

infant mortality the annual number of deaths of children under 1 year old for every thousand births. Ranges from under 10 in Western Europe to well over 100 in many parts of Africa and Asia.

life expectancy the average number of years a baby can expect to live when it is born. Europeans can expect to live over 70 years and Africans only about 50 years.

literacy the ability to read and write, providing access to education, skills and better jobs. Literacy is generally lower in developing countries, and fewer women than men are literate.

population structure the relative numbers of young and old people in the population. In developing countries with high birth rates, the young greatly outnumber the old.

population structure the relative numbers of young and old people in the population. In developing counties with high birth rates, the young greatly outnumber the old.

social security state system, funded by taxation, providing support and care for old, sick and unemployed people.

INDEX

Photographic Credits:
Cover and page 33: Zefa; intro page and pages 22 bottom, 23, 24 and 30/31 top: Panos Pictures; pages 4 bottom, 8 middle, 9 bottom, 19 and 27: Topham Picture Library; pages 5 top, 21 bottom and 33: Hutchison Library; pages 6 bottom, 18 and 19: Rex Features; pages 7 top and bottom, 8 bottom, 14, 22, 26, 27 and 30: Network Photographers; pages 9 top, 10 bottom, 16 top, 17, 20/21 and 25: Magnum Photos; page 11 bottom: Frank Lane Agency; page 13 top: Mary Evans Picture Library; page 17: Science Photo Library; page 28: Frank Spooner Agency; page 24: Unicef.